Earth's Changing Continents

by Neil Morris

Raintree

Chicago, Illinois

© Copyright 2004 Raintree
Published by Raintree, a division of Reed
Elsevier, Inc.
Chicago, IL 60602
Customer Service 888-363-4266
Visit our website at www.raintreelibrary.com

For more information address the publisher
Raintree, 100 N. LaSalle, Suite 1200, Chicago IL
60602

Printed and bound in China by South China
Printing Company
07 06 05 04 03
10 9 8 7 6 5 4 3 2 1

Editorial: Keith Ulrich
Design: Erica Barraca
Picture Services: Michelle Lisseter and Bridge
Creative Ltd
Illustrations: Bridge Creative Services Ltd
Production: Sal D'Amico

Acknowledgments
The publishers would like to thank the following
for permission to reproduce photographs:
p. 12 Christer Fredriksson/Bruce Coleman
Collection, p. 19 Staffan Widstrand/Bruce
Coleman Collection; p. 7 James A. Sugar/Corbis,
p. 11 Wild County/Corbis, p. 13 (top) Lloyd
Cluff/Corbis, p. 24 David Turnley/Corbis, p. 29
Tom Wagner/Corbis; p. 10 John Shaw/ NHPA, p.
15 Norbert Wu/NHPA; p. 14 David
Cayless/Oxford Scientific Films; p. 22 Sipa
Press/Rex Features, p. 23 Peter MacDiarmid/Rex
Features; p. 5 Dynamic Earth Imaging/Science
Photo Library, p. 9 Worldsat
International/Science Photo Library, p. 27 John
Beatty/Science Photo Library; p. 18 Werner
Foreman Archive.

**Library of Congress Cataloging-in-Publication
Data**

Morris, Neil, 1946-
  Earth's changing continents / Neil Morris.
    p. cm. -- (Landscapes and people)
Summary: Looks at the geography and people
that characterize the continents of the Earth,
focusing on the changing characteristics of
each.
Includes bibliographical references (p.   ) and
index.
  ISBN 1-4109-0179-3 (hc), 1-4109-0342-7(pb)
  1. Continents--Juvenile literature. 2. Landscape
changes--Juvenileliterature. 3. Ecology--Juvenile
literature. 4. Nature--Effect of human beings on-
-Juvenile literature. [1. Continents. 2. Landscape
changes. 3. Ecology. 4. Nature--Effect of human
beings on.] I. Title.
CURR G133.M69 2003
    910--dc21   2004

                                2003002173

Cover photograph of fully dark (city lights) image
centerd on Europe reproduced with permission of
Marit Jentoft-Nilsen, VAL, NASA GSFC.

The publishers would like to thank
Margaret Mackintosh for her assistance
in the preparation of this book.

Contents

Any words appearing in the text in bold, **like this,**
are explained in the Glossary.

What Is a Continent?

The town or city where you live is part of a state. In turn the state belongs to a larger region called a country. Did you know that every country also forms part of an even bigger area, called a continent?

We use the word continent to describe one of the world's main large areas of land. There are seven continents altogether, and some of these huge land masses are connected to each other. In order of size, from biggest to smallest, the world's continents are: Asia, Africa, North America, South America, Antarctica, Europe, and Australia. Some people refer to Australia, New Zealand, Papua New Guinea, and the thousands of small Pacific islands as Oceania or Australasia.

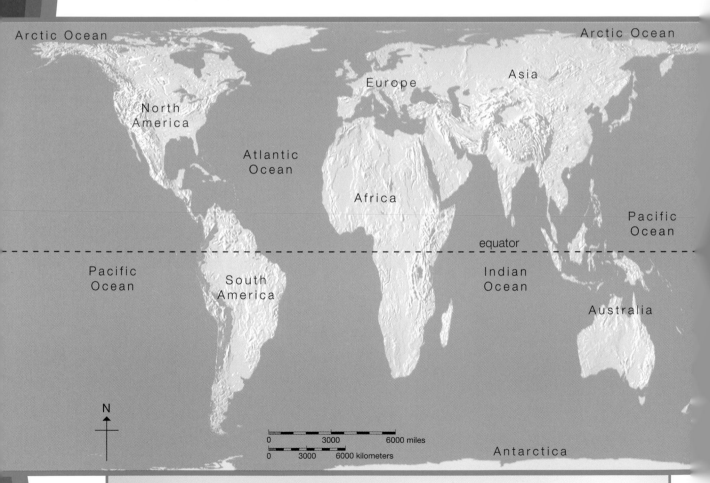

The southern continent of Antarctica is at the bottom of the world map. At the top the Arctic region is made up of frozen ocean and the most northerly parts of North America, Europe, and Asia.

Separated by oceans

Five oceans lie between the world's continents: the Pacific, Atlantic, Indian, Southern, and Arctic Oceans. The oceans are so big that their waters cover more than two-thirds of Earth's surface. The world's largest ocean, the Pacific, is just under four times as big as the world's largest continent, Asia.

Looking at continents

Earth's continents were formed millions of years ago. Since then they have been constantly, but very slowly, changing. They are home to millions of different kinds of plants and animals. People have tried to control the land they live on, and we continue to change the continents.

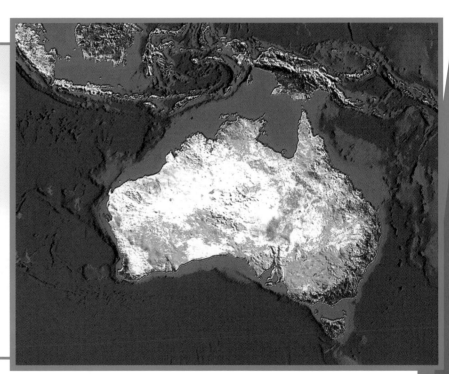

This satellite photograph shows the large land mass of Australia, the smallest of the seven continents. It is the worlds flattest and driest landmass, after Antarctica.

Linked continents

Some of the continents are linked. For example, a narrow strip of land, which we call Central America, joins the continents of North America and South America. Together, the continents of Europe and Asia form an even larger land mass, called Eurasia. Europe and Asia are divided by a range of mountains called the Urals. Asia is also linked to Africa by a piece of land called the Sinai peninsula. Large oceans separate the other continents.

How Did the Continents Form?

Scientists believe that Earth came into existence about 46 billion years ago. When it was first formed, the planet was red hot and the surface was covered with **volcanoes.** The volcanoes let off masses of steam, like a boiling kettle does, and when the steam cooled, it fell back to Earth as rain. There was so much rain that it collected into huge pools that eventually became one big, deep ocean.

Earth's outer layer

Beneath the deep ocean, our planet had a rocky outer layer, which today we call Earth's **crust.** The crust became harder as the planet gradually cooled down. The crust is not one continuous layer, like the shell of an egg or the peel of an orange. It is cracked into huge pieces, called **plates.** Earth's plates fit together like a giant jigsaw puzzle with the two sides of each plate close up against each other.

This map shows the world's major plates. As they move they change the shape of continents.

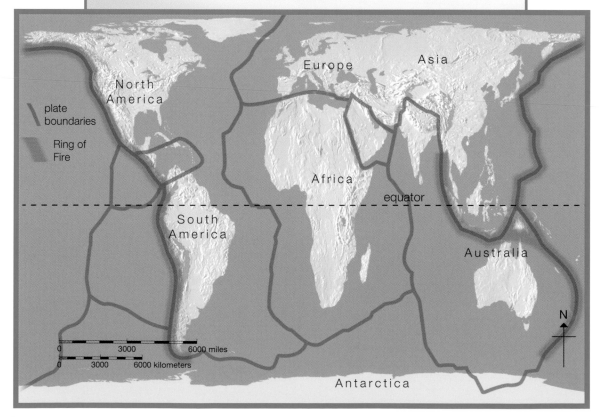

Continental plates

There are two types of plates—continental and oceanic. As their name suggests, continental plates are the ones with dry land on them. They form the continents that we are looking at in this book. The rocks that make up continental plates are very old and were mainly formed over 25 billion years ago. Continental plates are also thick—about 25 miles (40 kilometers) thick on average, reaching up to 49 miles (80 kilometers) beneath high mountain ranges. Oceanic plates make up the **seabed** of the world's oceans. Oceanic plates are younger than continental plates, generally less than 200 million years old. They are also thinner—an average of 6 miles (10 kilometers) thick.

◄ *Beneath Earth's crust the rock is so hot it has melted. At the edges of plates, this **molten** rock, called **magma,** sometimes forces its way through an opening in the crust. This makes a volcano.*

Supercontinent

Many millions of years ago, separate continental **plates** drifted together and joined up in one piece. The land then formed one huge continent, called a supercontinent. The supercontinent was surrounded by a single ocean. The scientist who discovered this called the supercontinent Pangaea (from the Greek for "all earth") and the huge ocean Panthalassa ("all sea").

Drifting apart

Around 200 million years ago, Pangaea split into two continents that began to move slowly apart. Scientists call the northern large continent Laurasia, and the southern continent Gondwanaland. Over millions of years, the continents went on splitting until they formed the land masses that we know today. This movement is called continental drift, because the continents slowly drifted

Laurasia split up into North America, Europe, and Asia. Gondwanaland became South America, Africa, Oceania, and Antarctica. The land that is now India was once part of the southern continent, but it broke away and drifted to the north, becoming part of Asia. This map shows what the continents looked like about 250 million years ago.

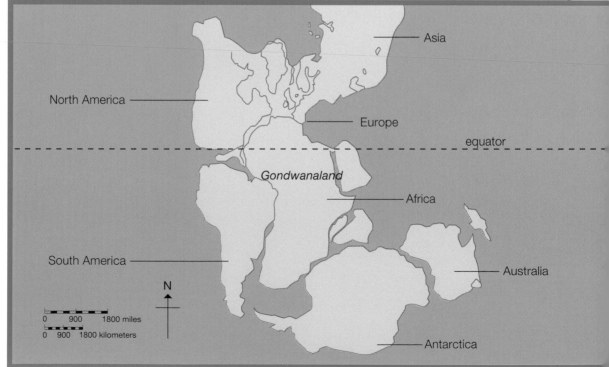

apart. These changes are still going on—for example, North America and Europe continue to move apart by just a few inches every year.

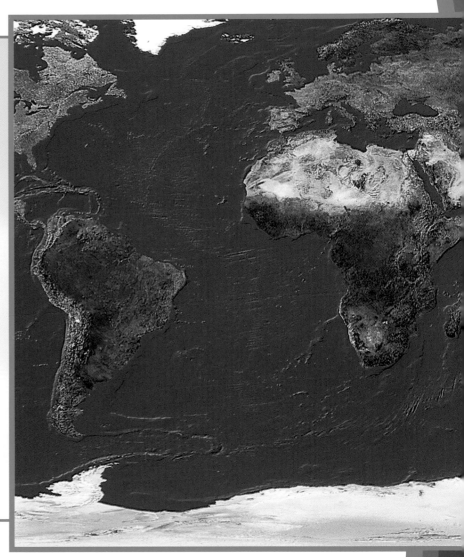

The easiest way to see how the continents split apart is to look at the east coast of South America and the west coast of Africa. Can you see how they would fit together? Today they are divided by the Atlantic Ocean. A huge underwater mountain range, called the Mid-Atlantic Ridge, stretches down the middle of the ocean. This is where new crust is created, pushing the continents apart.

Moving and scraping

Earth's plates are not still—they are always moving, very slowly, by just a few inches each year. Some move toward each other, others move apart, and some move past each other. When they push against each other, the plates buckle (bend) at the edges. It is this action that pushes mountain ranges up. The rubbing action of plates pushing against one another has another important effect. It creates **volcanoes** and **earthquakes,** which mainly occur at the edges of plates. There are mountain ranges on the ocean floor, too, but these are formed in a different way. As two plates move apart, **magma** comes to the surface and cools to form new **crust.**

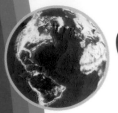

Changing Landscapes

All of Earth's hard, solid **crust** is made of rocks. In many places the rocks that make up the world's continents are covered with soil. This soil contains tiny bits of rock, as well as the rotting remains of dead plants and animals. In other places, especially high up in the mountains or near the coast, there is no soil and the rocks are bare. There are many different kinds of rocks, but they are all made of solid substances called **minerals.** The color of a rock, as well as its hardness and weight, depend on the minerals in it.

Forming different rocks

There are three main groups of rocks. They take their names from the way in which they are formed. **Sedimentary** rocks, such as sandstone, are made up of layers of sediment (tiny particles of rock). These build up on top of one another and are squeezed together until they harden into rock. Other rocks, such as granite, harden from hot **magma** (see page 7). These rocks are called **igneous** (meaning "fiery"). The third kind of rocks are called

Sedimentary rocks are formed in layers, called **strata.** *As* **plates** *move and mountains are forced up, the strata get folded. In the mountains and at the* **coast,** *you can often see the exposed strata. They look like wavy lines, as shown here at Wave Rock in Australia.*

metamorphic (meaning "changing form"). These rocks are changed by being heated or squashed. The metamorphic rock called quartzite, for example, is a changed form of sandstone.

The rock cycle

Although we think of rocks as the solid ground beneath our feet, they also change over time. In fact, rocks change in a never-ending cycle. **Volcanoes** throw out **molten** rock, which we call **lava.** The lava cools and hardens into solid rock. Over many years the effects of the weather wear this rock away in a process called erosion. Wind and rain break off bits of rock, which rivers carry to the ocean. There the rock particles settle on the ocean floor, pile up, and form layers of sediments that, over time, become new rocks. At the same time, heat inside the earth melts more rocks into magma, which is thrown out by volcanoes. This starts the rock cycle all over again.

The metamorphic rock called marble is a changed form of limestone. Marble is a valuable rock, used in buildings and sculptures. These blocks of white marble blocks have been cut out of a quarry in Carrara, Italy.

Higher and lower land

Much of the land that makes up the continents is hilly or mountainous. Mountains change little during a single human lifetime, but they change a great deal over thousands and millions of years. Some mountain ranges, such as the Himalayas in Asia, are still being pushed higher. The Himalayan range was formed when the land that eventually became India drifted north (see page 8) and finally bumped into Asia. Other mountain ranges are very slowly getting lower.

The Appalachians in the eastern United States were pushed up about 300 million years ago. At that time the land that became North America was a separate mass before becoming part of the supercontinent, Pangaea. At one time the Appalachians had high, jagged peaks. Since that time the peaks have been worn away to make more gentle and rounded slopes.

Where land meets ocean

All the continents have long coastlines, where the land meets the ocean. At the edge of every continent, there is a **continental shelf,** where the water is shallow. Here the **seabed** slopes gently away from the shore. Farther away from land and out to the ocean, the shelf turns into a steeper **continental slope.** Even farther out, there

The snowy peaks of the Himalayas tower above this valley in Nepal. The world's highest mountains are in this range.

is a thick pile of sand and mud called a **continental rise.** Beyond that is the deep floor of the ocean. The region from land to deep ocean is called a **continental margin.**

❝ When you look out to sea, the water seems to change color farther out. This is because the water is deeper over the continental shelf.

Great Rift Valley

Near the coast of East Africa, there is a series of deep cracks in the earth's **crust** known as the Great Rift Valley. The Rift Valley is about 4,470 miles (7,200 kilometers) long, stretching from Syria in the north to Mozambique in the south. It runs all the way across the boundary between the continents of Asia and Africa. The valley was formed about 30 million years ago by the movement of **plates.** These are still moving today, and scientists believe that in millions of years' time the part of Africa east of the Great Rift Valley may separate from the rest of Africa.

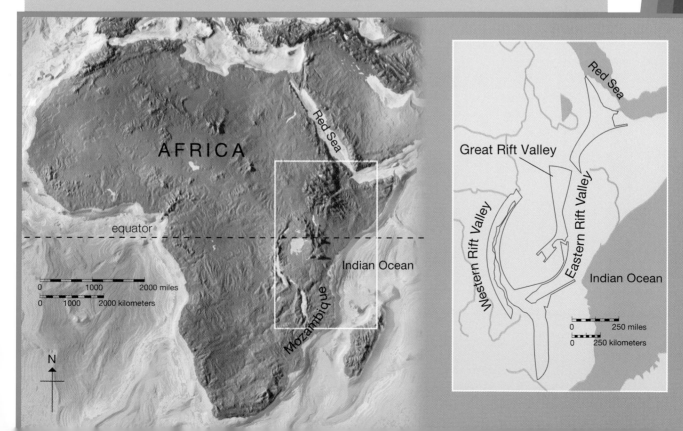

Changing Life

Changes in the position of the continents long ago had a great effect on the development of plants and animals. When the continents were all joined together as one single supercontinent (see page 8), land animals could walk all over Earth's land without having to cross any oceans. When the supercontinent split up, animals spread around the world with the shifting continents. This was how the giant **reptiles** called dinosaurs managed to spread around the world. Dinosaurs dominated life on Earth until they suddenly died out about 65 million years ago.

Cut-off continents

As the continents drifted apart, plants and animals developed in different ways on different land masses. This took place many millions of years ago, long before there were any humans on Earth. Today, Australia provides a good example of separate development.

This large land mass broke away from Antarctica and the rest of Gondwanaland about 50 million years ago. Since then it has been surrounded by ocean, and its animals and plants have developed in their own way. When European explorers first arrived in Australia just a few hundred years ago, they were amazed at the wildlife they found. They said it was a land where "birds ran instead of flying and animals hopped instead of running."

⟨ *The spider monkeys of Central and South America are experts at using their tails to hang on to trees.*

Kangaroos and koalas

Australia's running birds are emus, which are similar to the ostriches of Africa. The hopping animals are kangaroos, which are the best known of Australia's marsupials. These are animals whose young develop in pouches on their mother's body. There are 60 different kinds of kangaroos in Australia, and most of them are not found anywhere else in the world. Another famous marsupial is the koala. It looks a bit like a gray teddy bear, but it is not really related to bears and is only found in Australia.

Monkeys

The continents of South America and Africa were once attached. Today, some of the wildlife of the two continents are similar, but not exactly the same. South American monkeys, for example, have their nostrils spaced wide apart, while those of their African cousins are close together. The most interesting difference between them is that most South American monkeys use their grasping tail as a fifth limb, to swing through the trees. African monkeys do not.

Different habitats

Scientists divide the world into a number of different kinds of environment, or **habitats.** Each has its own collection of plants and animals that have **adapted** to life there. The habitats are greatly affected by the **climate,** or typical weather conditions, of the particular region. Regions close to the **equator,** which runs through South America, Africa, and southeast Asia, are hottest. Those nearest the North and South Poles, especially the continent of Antarctica in the south, are coldest. In between these two extremes, there are mild regions. The different environments on all the continents are also affected by how high above sea level the particular region is and how near it is to the **coast.**

> *This map shows how different vegetation is spread in regions across the continents. Most continents have many of the different types of vegetation. North America, for example, has eight types.*

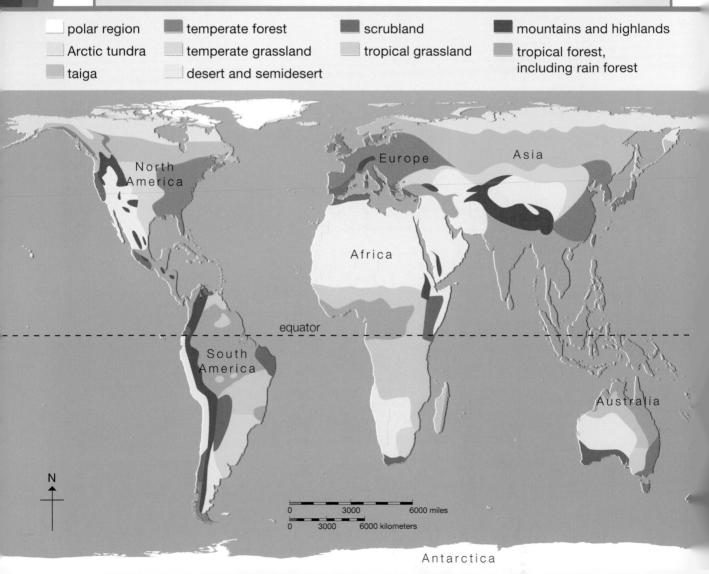

- polar region
- Arctic tundra
- taiga
- temperate forest
- temperate grassland
- desert and semidesert
- scrubland
- tropical grassland
- mountains and highlands
- tropical forest, including rain forest

North America

Europe

Asia

Africa

equator

South America

Australia

N

| 0 | 3000 | 6000 miles |
| 0 | 3000 | 6000 kilometers |

Antarctica

Life in the tropical rain forest

There are great similarities between the tropical **rain forests** of South America, Africa, and Asia. The biggest of them all, the Amazon rain forest of South America, has the greatest number of plants and animals. Scientists believe that up to one-tenth of all the world's **species** of animals and plants may live there, including up to one-fifth of all bird species.

Around the world

Different habitats stretch across the continents in bands (see the map on page 16). You can see this very well if you look at tropical grasslands and **deserts.** One huge forest stretches for 6,250 miles (10,000 kilometers) across the northern regions of Europe and Asia, from the Baltic Sea in the west to the Pacific Ocean in the east. This is the world's biggest forest, called taiga (from a Russian word). It continues across North America, covering about half the land area of Canada. North of the forest, in all three continents, is the frozen, treeless Arctic region. To the south are the warmer grasslands of the **steppes** in Russia, and the plains in Canada and the United States.

The largest floral kingdom on the planet is the boreal (northern) kingdom, which stretches across North America, Europe, and northern and central Asia.

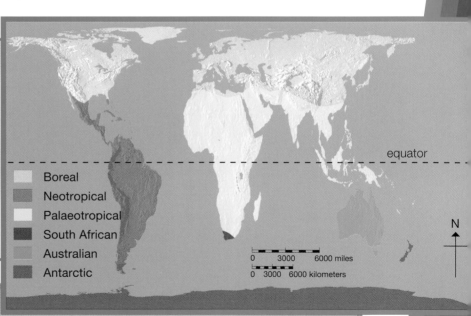

equator

Boreal
Neotropical
Palaeotropical
South African
Australian
Antarctic

0   3000   6000 miles
0 3000 6000 kilometers

N

Floral kingdoms

Flowering plants first appeared on Earth about 140 million years ago, when the continents were drifting apart. They have developed in different ways around the world. Scientists divide the world into six different regions, which are sometimes called floral kingdoms. There have been three main causes for the different regions: the way the continents drifted apart, climate in the past and today, and the way the individual plants adapted and developed.

Changing Settlements

People live on six of the seven continents of the world. Some scientists visit the frozen continent of Antarctica and work there, but no one lives there all the time. Unlike animals and plants, there were no human beings on Earth when the continents split apart many millions of years ago. So how did our **ancestors** manage to **populate** the whole planet?

Out of Africa

Some scientists believe that humanlike creatures, called **hominids,** first appeared in east Africa about six million years ago. That sounds like a very long time, but if you imagine the whole of Earth's history as just one day, hominids existed for the equivalent of less than two minutes! Modern humans developed from hominids and appeared in Africa over 100,000 years ago. That's the equivalent of just two seconds ago, when compared with Earth's one day and the hominids' two minutes. Some modern humans traveled north, first to Asia and Europe, and began the movement that finally took people around the whole world.

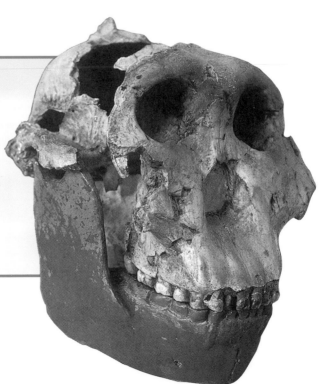

Scientists have learned a lot about our human history from fossils and bones. Many of these have been found in Africa. This skull was found in Tanzania, and is well over a million years old.

The Ice Age

During the time when humans were moving around the world, the **climate** was very cold. Much more of the world was covered in ice than it is today, which is why we call that period the Ice Age. As water turned to ice, sea levels went down around the globe. This meant that people could walk between different land masses. It is thought that the original peoples of Australia, the Aborigines, arrived there around 40,000 years ago. Sea levels were lower and there was more dry land, but the earliest people must still have used rafts to cross channels up to 80 miles (130 kilometers) wide.

Some Inuit people in northern Canada and Greenland still follow tradition and use kayaks to hunt and fish.

Native Americans

Many scientists believe that the first Americans were hunters from Asia, who crossed the Bering Strait to present-day Alaska about 17,000 years ago. There was then a strip of land between the two continents, which has since been covered by water as ice melted. These people probably stayed near the coast as they headed down toward South America. Some may have followed the course of rivers, knowing that there would always be fish and other animals there to catch and eat. Eventually they spread out across North and South America.

Farming and industry

The world's first people were **hunter-gatherers**. When people started to stay in one place and form **settlements** thousands of years ago, they became farmers. A few hundred years ago, many parts of the world went through an **Industrial Revolution,** when people began using machines, metals, and other **resources** to manufacture things.

Changing populations

In the last few centuries, the **populations** of different continents have changed rapidly. In 1790, when the first census (official count) was made, the United States had a population of four million. Most people had settled near the east coast and along the country's rivers. Since then huge numbers of people came to North America from other continents. This is called immigration, and it resulted in the growth of towns and cities as the United States became an industrial nation. Today the population is about 280 million, and about 2 million of these people are Native Americans. Three-quarters of the U.S. population live in towns and cities.

> ❮ *This map shows the U.S., with the number of people living in each state. Two states are not shown: Alaska has a population of 552,000 and Hawaii has 1,115,000 people.*

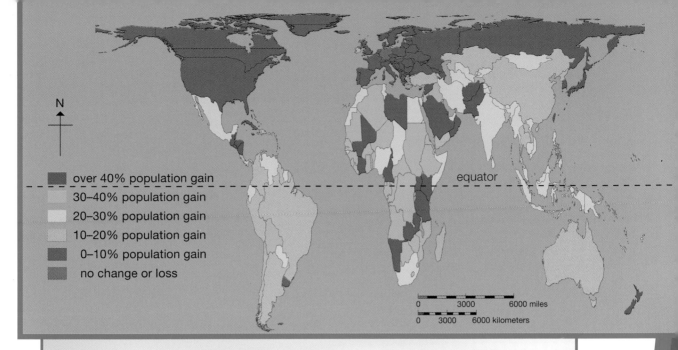

over 40% population gain
30–40% population gain
20–30% population gain
10–20% population gain
0–10% population gain
no change or loss

equator

0   3000   6000 miles
0   3000   6000 kilometers

This map shows how population grew across the world in the ten years between 1990 and 2000. While Canada and the United States had a very low increase, Mexico and the countries of Central America increased rapidly.

The population explosion

Over the last 50 years, there has been a population explosion. In that time the number of people in the world has more than doubled, and now totals more than six billion. In 1950 less than one-third of people lived in towns. By 2000 the number had grown to almost half, and it is expected to be around two-thirds by 2025. As you can see from the map above, the population explosion is greatest in Africa. South America and Asia are also high, while Europe is very low, with practically no increase.

Lake Victoria

People settle where there are natural resources to help them with their lives. Water is a precious resource, because it is needed for drinking, washing, and watering farmland. Rivers, lakes, and oceans also have fish |in them, which can be caught for food. Lake Victoria is the largest lake in Africa and the third largest in the world. Its shores are divided among the countries of Tanzania, Uganda, and Kenya. Millions of people live near the shores of this lake. Ships link the main ports of Mwanza in Tanzania, Entebbe in Uganda, and Kisumu in Kenya.

Living on the edge

Extreme weather can cause natural disasters around the world, but some continents are in more danger than others. Hurricanes are large, powerful storms with high winds that cause great damage when they pass over land. They start over warm ocean waters in regions near the **equator.** Atlantic hurricanes mostly affect the Caribbean islands, Mexico, and other Central American countries, and the southeast corner of North America. Tropical storms in the Pacific Ocean are known as typhoons (from the Chinese for "great winds"), and they often hit eastern Asia. In and around the Indian Ocean, these storms are called cyclones, or tornados.

Floods in Bangladesh

Some regions of continents are at higher risk because of their location. The coastal region of Bangladesh, in southern Asia, lies directly in the path of many cyclones that move in from the Indian Ocean. Water also runs off the Himalaya Mountains to this area of flat land around the **delta** of the Ganges River, and it is easily flooded. Almost every year thousands of Bangladeshis are made homeless by floods. In 1998, floods in two-thirds of the country claimed about 900 lives and left 30 million people homeless.

These Bangladeshi people were among the millions who stood in line for food after they lost their homes in the 1998 flood.

Volcanoes and earthquakes

Volcanic eruptions and **earthquakes** can also cause terrible disasters all over the world. Active **volcanoes** lie at the edge of Earth's **plates** (see page 6), and a large number of them form a huge belt around the Pacific Ocean. This belt is known as the "Ring of Fire," and earthquakes are very common along its whole length. It affects people on four continents around the world's largest ocean: Asia, North America, South America, and Australia.

The town of Bhachau, in northwest India, was left in ruins after a powerful earthquake struck in 2001. Tens of thousands of people were killed here and in nearby villages.

Living on faults

There are thousands of minor earthquakes all over the world every year, but the state of California has some big ones. They happen because the Pacific coast of California lies along the San Andreas **Fault,** which is 650 miles (1,050 kilometers) long. It is the place where two plates are sliding past each other at the rate of about 2 inches (5 centimeters) each year. In 1994 the town of Northridge, 19 miles (30 kilometers) north of Los Angeles, shook for 20 seconds. This earthquake killed 57 people, and over 20,000 were left homeless.

Changing Continents

Apart from Antarctica all of the world's continents are divided up into countries. In 2003 there were 193 separate countries on 6 continents, but the total number often changes as nations join together or divide. On most continents neighboring countries try to help each other, because they face similar challenges. In Europe, for example, many countries are joined together in the European Union, which makes it easier for member countries to trade with each other.

Natural resources

Some of the world's natural **resources** are essential for people's survival. Most of these, including the air that we breathe and the water that we drink, are available on all continents. People's lives have developed in different ways on different continents, however, and there is no longer a balance between them. Generally, the northern continents are much wealthier than the southern ones.

Their lifestyles cause them to use more of the world's resources, including fresh water. For example, North Americans are generally richer than South Americans, and Europeans are generally better off than Africans. Many of the world's aid agencies are working hard to help the poorer nations. They are trying to make sure that every continent has basic standards of food, housing, and education.

This woman is farming in Tanzania, east Africa. On average, people here have to pay more than 5 percent of their wages for the fresh water they need every day. In Europe and North America, people pay much less than 1 percent of their wages for fresh water.

Oil

Oil is one of the world's most important natural resources. It is used to power factories and cars, as well as to make plastics and many other products. There are known oil reserves on all the world's continents, and oil has been a very useful resource to some of the poorer nations in South America and Africa. The first oil well was drilled in Pennsylvania in 1859. More than 80 years later, oil was discovered beneath the Arabian **Desert** in southwest Asia. The discovery brought wealth to the region and its largest country, Saudi Arabia, is the world's leading producer of crude oil. Scientists have estimated that more than half the world's oil reserves are in this desert region.

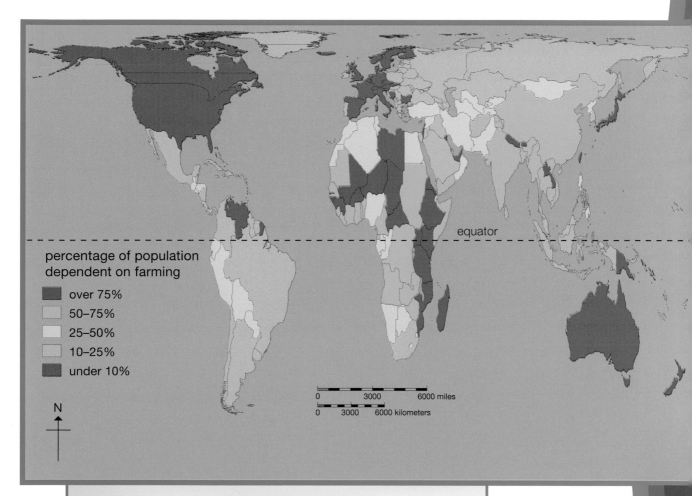

percentage of population
dependent on farming

- over 75%
- 50–75%
- 25–50%
- 10–25%
- under 10%

equator

0   3000   6000 miles
0   3000   6000 kilometers

N

The map shows the importance of farming in today's world. Many people depend on farming in Africa and Asia, while fewer people do in North America, Europe, and Australia.

The changing climate

Generally the world's **climate** is heating up by a very small amount each year. Many scientists believe that the warming is partly caused by the greenhouse effect, which is created by heat-trapping gases. These gasses trap the earth's heat, like the glass of a greenhouse. The gases we release by burning fuel, such as the exhaust fumes given off by cars, add to this effect. It may cause a general increase in temperature called global warming. In turn, this may make the land drier and even cause **deserts** to spread.

Rising sea levels

Many scientists believe that ice at the North and South Poles is melting because the global temperature is rising. Eventually this will mean that sea levels will rise around the world. This will change the shape of the coastlines around all the continents, flooding existing land near the shore.

> *This map shows how the world's coastlines might change if all the ice at the North and South Poles melted.*

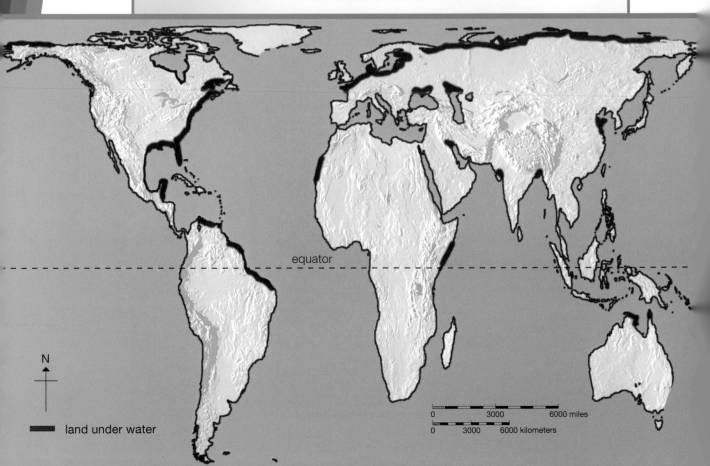

equator

N

land under water

0   3000   6000 miles
0   3000   6000 kilometers

Scientists from around the world gather together at the Amundsen-Scott research station at the South Pole in Antarctica. At the southernmost point on Earth, these scientists are learning more about the ozone layer. They also study the Antarctic ice cap, to see if it is being affected by global warming.

Above the southern continent

Earth is protected from some of the sun's harmful rays by a layer of gas high in the atmosphere called ozone. In recent years a hole has appeared in the ozone layer over Antarctica, the frozen continent around the South Pole. Scientists believe that the ozone was partly attacked by gases called CFCs, which have been widely used in aerosol sprays, refrigerators, and fast-food packages. The countries of the world have agreed to reduce the use of these gases. If the ozone hole gets much bigger, Antarctic animals like seals and penguins might be endangered. Temperatures would probably rise and some of the frozen continent's ice would start to melt. This could affect all the other continents.

Into the future

The continents will always keep changing, but most of the changes will be gradual and take place over many years. Some of the changes will be due to natural forces, like the movement of Earth's **plates.** Others will be due to the actions of humans using up Earth's natural **resources.** We also use more and more land on all the continents, making it difficult for some animals and plants to survive. We must hope that the world's people will work together to make future changes positive and valuable.

Continent Facts and Figures

Size of continents and their largest countries					
continent	area sq miles	area sq km	largest country	area sq miles	area sq km
Asia	17,225,562	44,614,000	China*	3,696,117	9,572,900
Africa	11,631,714	30,216,000	Sudan	966,761	2,503,900
North America	9,355,255	24,230,000	Canada	3,851,794	9,976,100
South America	6,878,024	17,814,000	Brazil	3,265,073	8,456,500
Antarctica	5,500,025	14,245,000	—	—	—
Europe	4,056,003	10,505,000	Ukraine*	233,090	603,700
Australia	3,283,027	8,503,000	Australia	2,966,153	7,682,300

*Russia (partly in Europe and Asia) is the biggest country in the world
(8,442,162 sq miles/21,347,100 sq km).

Population of continents and their most populous countries			
continent	pop in millions	country	pop in millions
Asia	3.672	China	1.285
Africa	794	Nigeria	112
Europe	727	Germany*	82
North America	487	United States	278
South America	346	Brazil	170
Australasia	31	Australia	19

*Russia (part of which is in Europe) has a population of 147 million.

Growth of population

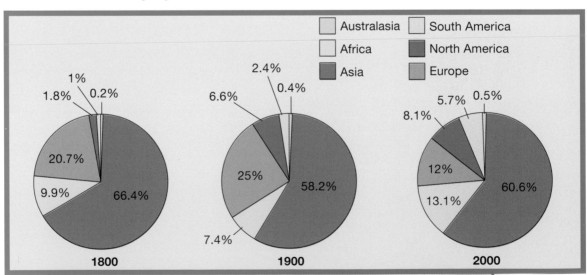

These charts show the percentage of the world's people on six continents in 1800, 1900, and 2000. Antarctica has stayed at zero.

28

Most populous cities

continent	city	country	pop in millions
Asia	Tokyo	Japan	26.4
North America	Mexico City	Mexico	18.1
South America	São Paulo	Brazil	18.0
Europe	Paris	France	9.6
Africa	Cairo	Egypt	9.5
Australia	Sydney	Australia	3.8

Worst earthquakes of the 20th century

location	country	continent	date	number of people killed
Tangshan	China	Asia	1976	242,000
Xining	China	Asia	1927	200,000
Gansu	China	Asia	1920	180,000
Tokyo	Japan	Asia	1923	143,000
Messina	Italy	Europe	1908	100,000
Gansu	China	Asia	1932	80,000
Yungay	Peru	S. America	1970	67,000
Quetta	Pakistan	Asia	1935	50,000
Roudhon	Iran	Asia	1990	40,000
Armenia	Armenia	Asia	1988	25,000

◖ As this busy street suggests, Tokyo, in Japan, has the highest population of any city in the world.

Glossary

adapt to change in order to suit the conditions

ancestor person who lived long ago from whom someone is descended

climate usual weather conditions in a particular area

coast edge of land where it meets the ocean

continental margin whole region of the continental shelf, slope, and rise

continental rise gently sloping pile of sand and mud at the edge of a continental slope, leading to the deep ocean

continental shelf area of gently sloping sea bed at the edge of a continent, where the water is shallow

continental slope steep slope at the edge of a continental shelf, farther out to sea

crust hard outer layer of Earth

delta fan-shaped area at the mouth of some rivers, where the river splits into many smaller channels

desert area of very dry land

earthquake sudden shaking of the ground caused by movements beneath Earth's surface

equator imaginary circle that stretches around the middle of Earth

fault crack in Earth's crust

habitat natural environment, or home, of an animal or plant

hominid one of several different kinds of human-like creatures that existed on Earth before modern humans

hunter-gatherer wandering person who lives by hunting, fishing, and collecting wild food such as roots and berries

igneous (rocks) made from cooled, solidified lava or magma

Industrial Revolution rapid development of machinery and factories that began in the late 1700s

lava hot, molten rock that pours out of a volcano onto Earth's surface

magma hot molten rock formed beneath Earth's surface

metamorphic (rocks) changed by great heat or pressure

mineral substance that occurs naturally on Earth

molten melted (turned into liquid by heat)

plate huge piece of Earth's crust

populate inhabit a place and usually to increase in number

population total number of people who live in a particular place

rain forest thick forest found in warm tropical areas of heavy rainfall

reptile scaly-skinned, cold-blooded animal like snakes, lizards, and crocodiles

resource supply of something that can be used

seabed ground under the sea; the ocean floor

sedimentary (rocks) formed from rock particles that have been moved and laid down by ice, water, or wind

settlement place where people live permanently

species type or kind of animal or plant

steppe flat, grassy plain (especially in Russia)

strata layers of rock

volcano opening where molten rock and gas come from deep inside Earth, often forming a mountain

Further Reading

Chambers, Catherine. *Mapping Earthforms: Oceans and Seas.* Chicago: Heinemann Library, 2000.

Hunter, Rebecca. *Discovering Geography: Volcanoes and Earthquakes.* Chicago: Raintree, 2003.

Stewart, Melissa. *Rocks and Minerals: Igneous Rocks.* Chicago: Heinemann Library, 2002.

Index